How to Submit iPhone and iPad Apps Successfully and Quickly:

Getting Your Application Submitted and Approved to The App Store Successfully With or Without Coding. Itunes, Xcode, and IOS Explanations and Solutions to Common Problems.

By
Joseph Correa

COPYRIGHT

This publication is designed to provide accurate and authoritative information in regard to the subject matter covered. It is sold with the understanding that neither the author nor the publisher is engaged in rendering advice. If technical assistance is needed, consult with an app specialist in the IT field that may address detailed issues. This book is considered a guide and should not be used in any way otherwise.

ACKNOWLEDGEMENTS

This book is dedicated to my family. Thank you for giving me the inspiration to make this book possible.

How to Submit iPhone and iPad Apps Successfully and Quickly:

Getting Your Application Submitted and Approved to The App Store Successfully With or Without Coding. Itunes, Xcode, and IOS Explanations and Solutions to Common Problems.

By
Joseph Correa

TABLE OF CONTENTS

INTRODUCTION

This book will teach you how to successfully submit an app to the Apple® app store and get it approved using a step by step process from start to finish. Learn how to open a developer account and become a registered Apple® developer. You will be taught how to create a distribution provisioning profile, an app archive, an app listing in Itunes and submitting your app using the Xcode.

Common mistakes are addressed and solutions to these mistakes are detailed to help you over come frustrating situations that might be easily fixed and corrected to get you through the app submission process successfully.

A step by step process will be explained in each chapter like this:

Chapter One: Registering for an Apple® Developer account

Chapter Two: Create a distribution provisioning profile

Chapter Three: Creating an app archive

Chapter Four: Creating app listing in iTunes connect portal

Chapter Five: App submission using the Xcode

Chapter Six: Common mistakes in the Apple® app submission and ways of preventing them

CHAPTER ONE

Registering for an Apple® Developer Account

The Apple® App store is a digital distribution platform for mobile Apps. There are a million apps in the App store and over 60 billion apps have been downloaded so far. Submitting your app for the iOS platform is easy. But, before we go into that, you need to ensure that:

1.   Your app name is short, simple and concise. Use nothing more than 25 characters.

2.   Make sure your app name doesn't violate the trademarks or rights of a third-party. For example, "iPhone game News" does not sound right, because "iPhone" is an Apple® trademark.

3.   Make it easy for people to discover your app across iOS platforms. Use the same app name on each platform.

4.   Don't use a similar app name with other existing apps.

5.   Make sure you write the app name below the app icon, so that customers can associate the app name with the icon.

Required tools / Resources
1.   The app
2.   US $99 registration fee
3.   A browser
4.   Internet connection
5.   A Mac computer

Although, being a registered iOS developer is a long process, you only need to go through it once. After that, you can submit as many apps as you want with your developer account.

There are five stages involved in app submission to the Apple® app store. They are:

1.   Registering for an Apple® Developer account
2.   Creating a distribution provisioning profile
3.   Building an app distribution provisioning profile
4.   Creating an app archive
5.   Creating app listing in iTunes connect portal
6.   App submission using Xcode

1. Registering for a Developer Account

The first step is to register as an App developer. You don't need to pay any fee to become an app developer. However, becoming an iOS developer attracts a fee of US$99 fee. If you already have a developer account with Apple®, you can skip this part and move to the next step.

If you don't have an Apple® developer account, you can have one by click on https://developer.apple.com/ and then
"M*ember center*" as shown below.

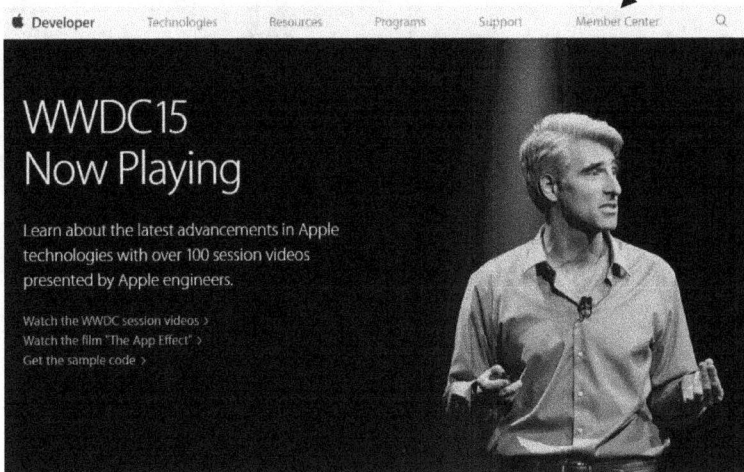

2. On the next screen, you can either register with an existing Apple® ID if you have one, or you can create an entirely new one. The benefit of registering with an already existing Apple® ID is that most of the information you will need for the developer account should already be stored with an existing ID, so you will not need to fill them again.

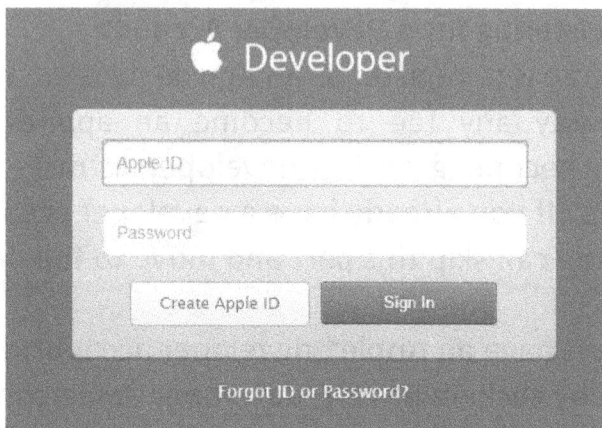

In case you do not have an Apple® ID, or you want a new ID strictly for app development, simply click on the *"Create Apple® ID"* link. Continue by filling all requested information such as your full names, your preferred Apple® ID (usually an email address), and a suitable password.

3.   After this, you will need to complete the form below. Make sure you use an email address you check often because Apple® sends regular updates on the program and on the status of the apps you submit for approval.

Create an Apple ID.

Name

Please enter your full name.

First Name

Middle Name   Optional

Last Name

Apple ID and Password

Enter your primary email address as your Apple ID. This will be used as the contact email address for your account.

Apple ID   example: jappleseed@example.com

Password

Confirm Password

Security Questions

Select three security questions below. These questions will help us verify your identity should you forget your password.

Security Question   Please select ▼

Answer

Security Question   Please select ▼

Answer

Security Question   Please select ▼

Answer

Date of Birth

Combined with your security question, this will help us verify your identity if you forget your password or need to reset it.

Month ▼   Day ▼   Year ▼

Rescue Email Address

Give us a rescue email address where we can send you a link to confirm your identity and let you reset your information should any security issues arise. This address is only for communicating information about your security details. We won't send any other types of messages to this address.

Rescue Email Address: Optional

Mailing Address

Please enter your mailing address.

Country/Region: United States

Company/Institution: Optional

Address Line 1:

Address Line 2: Optional

Town/City:

State/Province: Please select

Zip Code:

Email Preference

Stay up to date with Apple news, software updates, and the latest information about products and services from Apple. Please note. Email messages appear in the official language(s) of your country of residence. Read the Apple Customer Privacy Policy ▸

☑ **Apple News and Announcements**

Keep me up to date with Apple news, software updates, and the latest information on products and services.

☑ **New on iTunes and Other iTunes Offers**

Every week, iTunes adds the latest new releases for music, apps, movies, TV, books, podcasts, and much more — plus exclusive content you'll only find on iTunes. Sign up for New On iTunes and other iTunes offers.

Please type the characters you see in the image below.

1BD4Z

Ↄ Try a different image
◀) Vision Impaired

Letters are not case sensitive.

Cancel   Create Apple ID

4.   Immediately you are done with the registration, you will get an e-mail notification at the e-mail address you used during the registration, requesting you to verify your Apple® ID by clicking on an activation link within the notification message.

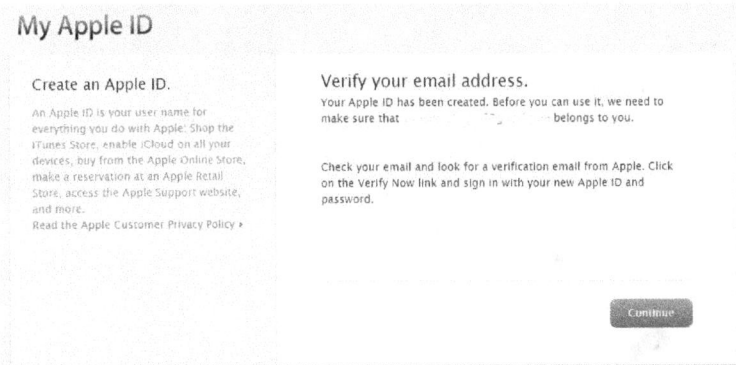

My Apple ID

Create an Apple ID.

An Apple ID is your user name for everything you do with Apple: Shop the iTunes Store, enable iCloud on all your devices, buy from the Apple Online Store, make a reservation at an Apple Retail Store, access the Apple Support website, and more.
Read the Apple Customer Privacy Policy ▸

Verify your email address.

Your Apple ID has been created. Before you can use it, we need to make sure that   belongs to you.

Check your email and look for a verification email from Apple. Click on the Verify Now link and sign in with your new Apple ID and password.

Continue

Open the activation e-mail, find the **Verify Now** activation link, and click on it.

After you have verified your Apple® ID, you will then complete the rest of your registration within your Apple® Developer account.

Now you have an Apple® ID. This implies that you are now an Apple® developer! But it doesn't mean you can start developing apps and submitting them to the app store. You have to join the iOS Developer program.

Join the iOS Developer Program

As a registered Apple® developer, you have certain privileges which include timely information for Apple®. However, you cannot submit an app to the app store without enrolling in Apple® iOS developer program. This is where you need to pay the US $99 per year.

5.   Log into your new Apple® Developer account.

6.   Read the License Agreement and call up your lawyer and read the whole agreement to him/her on the phone. When your lawyer gives you a go ahead, check the boxes, then click on submit.

7. On the next screen, "click on "Your account". Scroll down to the Membership area and click the **Enroll Now** link.

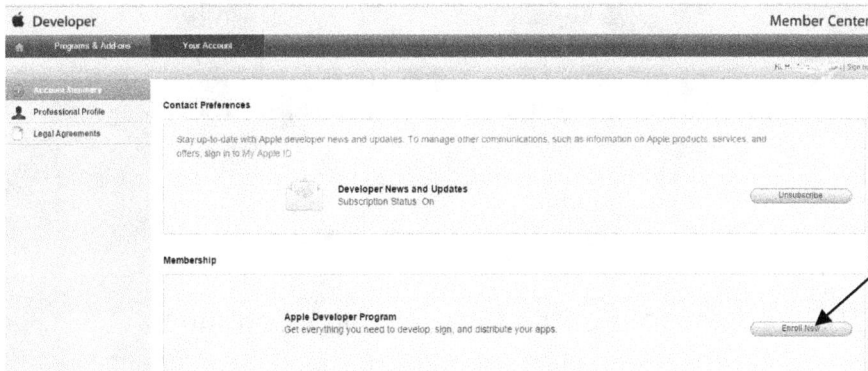

8. Next, click the **Start your Enrollment** link.

Apple Developer Program

What You Need to Enroll

Enrolling as an Individual

If you are an individual or sole proprietor/single person business, sign in with your Apple ID to get started. You'll need to provide basic personal information, including your legal name and address.

Enrolling as an Organization

If you're enrolling your organization, you'll need an Apple ID as well as the following to get started:

A D-U-N-S® Number

Your organization must have a D-U-N-S Number so that we can verify your organization's identity and legal entity status. These unique nine-digit numbers are assigned by Dun & Bradstreet and are widely used as standard business identifiers. You can check to see if your organization already has a D-U-N-S Number and request one if necessary. They are free in most jurisdictions. Learn more >

Legal Entity Status

Your organization must be a legal entity to so that it can enter into contracts with Apple. We do not accept DBAs, Fictitious Businesses, Trade names, or branches.

Legal Binding Authority

As the person enrolling your organization in the Apple Developer Program, you must have the legal authority to bind your organization to legal agreements. You must be the organization's owner/founder, executive team member, senior project lead, or have legal authority granted to you by a senior employee.

Start Your Enrollment

9. Fill in your **email, name, and country**.

Apple Developer Program Enrollment

Apple ID Information

The information on this Apple ID account will be used for verification and legal agreements, so please make sure your legal name and country are correct. To edit your account information, contact us.

Email

Name

Country

10. Select your entity type and click Continue

Entity Type

I develop apps as   Select

Select
Individual / Sole Proprietor / Single Person Business
Company / Organization
Government Organization

Cancel   Continue

Here, you have to choose whether you want to enroll as an individual or as a company. In this tutorial, we are enrolling as an individual, which is what most people do. However, if you choose to enroll as a company, the process is a bit difficult. You will need to provide a D-U-N-S number, and your company must be registered. You will need to submit a lot of paperwork to show that it is your company.

We will move on by clicking the "individual" entity.

11.   Fill in the form below with the required details.

Apple Developer Program Enrollment   Your Information

Sign out

Contact Information

The name on this Apple ID account will be used as your seller
name, and for contracts and banking, if your app is selected
for distribution by Apple. Make sure that it is your legal name
and that your country is correct. To edit your account
information, contact us.

Legal Name

Phone

Country Code   Phone Number   Extension

Enter your home or business address in your local language.

Address Line 1

Address Line 2
optional

Town / City

Postal Code
optional

Country   Ghana

12.   Read the Developer Program License agreement and check the appropriate boxes, then click on "**continue**"

Apple Developer Program License Agreement

This is a legal agreement between you and Apple.

☐ Download PDF

PLEASE READ THE FOLLOWING APPLE DEVELOPER PROGRAM LICENSE AGREEMENT TERMS AND CONDITIONS CAREFULLY BEFORE DOWNLOADING OR USING THE APPLE SOFTWARE OR APPLE SERVICES. THESE TERMS AND CONDITIONS CONSTITUTE A LEGAL AGREEMENT BETWEEN YOU AND APPLE.

Apple Developer Program License Agreement

Purpose

You would like to use the Apple Software (as defined below) to develop one or more Applications (as defined below) for Apple-branded products. Apple is willing to grant You a limited license to use the Apple Software and Services provided to You under this Program to develop and test Your Applications on the terms and conditions set forth in this Agreement.

Applications developed under this Agreement for iOS Products or Apple Watch can be distributed in four ways: (1) through the App Store, if selected by Apple, (2) through the B2B Program area of the App Store, if selected by Apple, (3) on a limited basis for use on Registered Devices (as defined below), and (4) for beta testing through TestFlight. Applications developed for OS X can be distributed through the App Store, if selected by Apple, or separately distributed under this Agreement.

Applications that meet Apple's Documentation and Program Requirements may be submitted for consideration by Apple for distribution via the App Store, B2B Program, or for beta testing through TestFlight. If submitted by You and selected by Apple, Your Applications will be digitally signed by Apple and distributed, as applicable. Distribution of free (no charge) Applications (including those that use the In-App Purchase API for the delivery of free content) will be subject to the distribution terms contained in Schedule 1 to this Agreement. If You would like to distribute Applications for which You will charge a fee or would like to use the In-App Purchase API for the delivery of fee-based content, You must enter into a separate agreement with Apple ("Schedule 2"). If You would like to distribute Applications via the B2B Program, You must enter into a separate agreement with Apple ("Schedule 3"). You may also create Passes (as defined below) for use on Apple-branded products running iOS or watchOS under this Agreement and distribute such

☐ By checking this box I confirm that I have read and agree to be bound by the Apple Developer Program License Agreement. I also confirm that I am of the legal age of majority in the jurisdiction in which I reside (at least 18 years of age in many countries).

Cancel   Back   Continue

A page that contains all your completed data will pop up.

13. Make payment for your developer's account by clicking on "**Purchase**," for a yearly fee of $99. Ensure you enter the right credit card information because Apple® will confirm the information you supplied with your credit card company.

14. Click on **Continue** after entering your payment details.

Enter your payment information.

Purchase items

☑ **Apple Developer Program** $99.00
  1 year membership

Your order will be charged in U.S. dollars.   **Order Total:** $99.00

Payment Information

Credit Card
Enter the number, cardholder's name, and expiration date for your credit card. We accept Visa, Mastercard, Discover, and American Express.

Type: [Select one ▼]

Number: [   ]   (A)

Cardholder's Name: [   ]

Expires: [▼] [▼]

Billing Information
Enter the billing information for your credit card.

Country: [Select Country ▼]

Address Line 1: [   ]

Address Line 2: [optional]   (B)

City/Town: [   ]

State, Province, or Region: [Select State ▼]

Postal Code: [   ]

Phone: [   ]

[Cancel]   [⟵]   (C)

Complete Your Purchase

Once you complete your purchase, you will receive a purchase acknowledgement and a membership confirmation email.

Membership	Apple Developer Program
Cost	US$ 99
Duration	1 year
Enrollment ID	P7AKQK2L2U

Cancel Purchase

You are done. You only need to wait for an e-mail from Apple® confirming your payment. The verification of your payment may take a while (usually a few days to 2 weeks), so do not expect the e-mail immediately.

Once your payment is confirmed, Apple® will automatically open an iTunes Connect account for you. This is because you need an iTunes connect account for app submission to the Apple® App Store. This account is different from your developer account.

If you are a company but do not know your D-U-N-S Number, you can easily get it through the DUNS Lookup Tool. You will be presented with a look-up form to fill your company's details. After you have completed this form, you will get an e-mail containing your company's D-U-N-S number, which is a 9-digit number used for business referencing.

On the iOS Developer enrollment form, at the section where you will be requested to **Enter Your organization**

Information, make sure you DO NOT enter your D-U-N-S number with the hyphens.

After entering your D-U-N-S number, you will be taken to another screen where you will be asked to verify your company's address. Review the details on this screen to make sure they are correct. If they are correct, continue with the enrollment process, if not, go back to the previous screen and make your corrections where needed.

Once you are okay with the company address and details you have entered, choose the type of developer program in which you are interested. Since your interest in the Apple® App Store is in the development of tablet/mobile Apps, choose the **iOS Developer Program only**.

Before you continue, review the enrollment details.

After you have reviewed all the enrollment details, you will be notified that your enrollment is undergoing processing.

The final steps you need to take in order to complete your enrollment process will be sent to your e-mail, and this will not be immediate.

Completing Your Enrollment Process

When you get the e-mail from Apple® confirming your signature mandate, all the remaining steps you need to finalize your iOS Developer enrollment will be contained in it.

CHAPTER TWO

Create a distribution provisioning profile

Here, we will build a distribution provisioning profile. With a developer profile, you have the flexibility of selecting many development certificates in order to enable many developers create a build. However, when you consider the iOS distribution provisioning profile, there is only enough room for one distribution certificate. This becomes the sole signing ID for code signing your app when you create the app archive (what you submit to the Apple® App Store).

You can now access the Distribution Provisioning Profiles section by logging into your iOS Developer Provisioning Portal .
At the top right corner, locate the **Plus** button, click it and create a new profile. Select **App Store** as your profile type and click **Continue.**

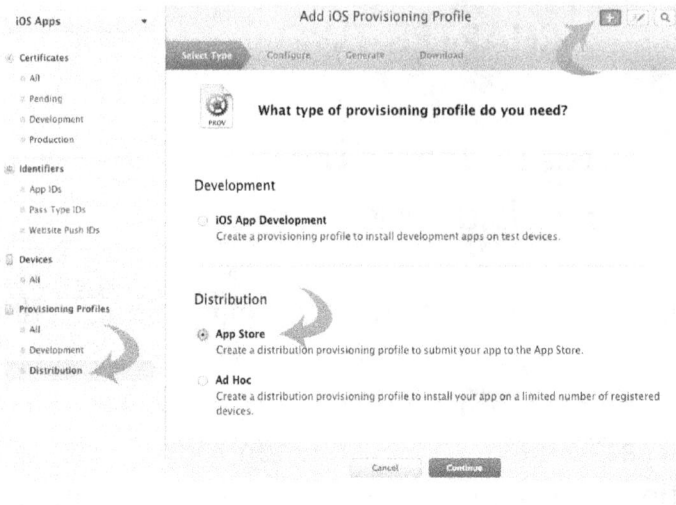

Click the drop down list and choose your App ID.

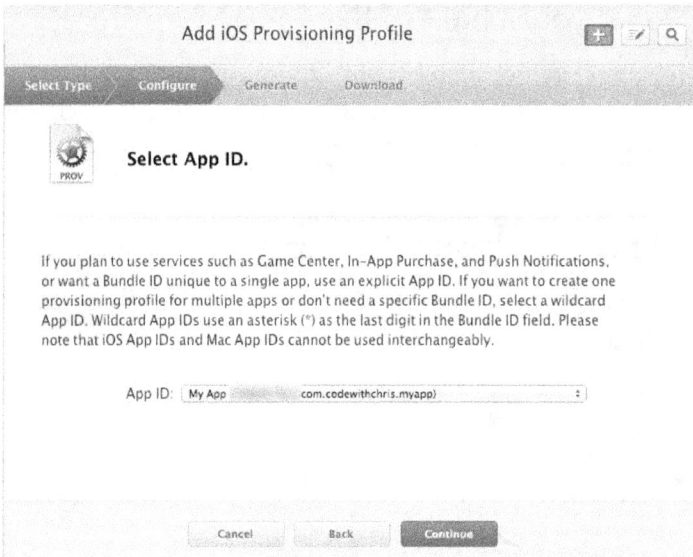

Here, you should see a **distribution certificate**. Select the **distribution certificate** and click **Continue**.

Add iOS Provisioning Profile

Select Type | Configure | Generate | Download

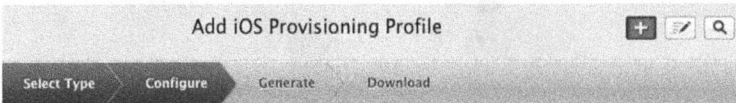

Select certificates.

Select the certificates you wish to include in this provisioning profile. To use this profile to install an app, the certificate the app was signed with must be included.

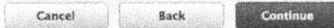

(iOS Distribution)

Cancel | Back | Continue

Give the profile a name and click on **Generate**.

Add iOS Provisioning Profile

Select Type | Configure | Generate | Download

Name this profile and generate.

The name you provide will be used to identify the profile in the portal. You cannot use special characters such as @, &, *, ', " for your profile name.

Profile Name: My App Distribution Profile

Type: Distribution

App ID: My App (com.   myapp)

Certificates: 1 Included

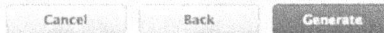

Cancel | Back | Generate

Download the profile and **install** by double clicking it

Your provisioning profile is ready.

Download and Install

Download and double click the following file to install your Provisioning Profile.

Name: My App Distribution Profile
Type: Distribution
App ID: .myapp
Expires: Sep 18, 2014

Download

CHAPTER THREE

Creating an app archive

First, open your app project in the Xcode environment. However, before we go any further in creating an archive for submission to iTunes Connect, we need to be certain that we have covered all the bases. This checklist will guide us to do the right things.

- Check if you have incorporated a splash image and app icon into your app.

- Does your app support iOS 6? If it does, have you run your app in an iOS 6 device and simulator to check for compatibility?

- Ensure to comment out every of your NSLog statements.

- Have you opened your app in a real device? How does your app behave during an incoming call, or when a user logs off the app and logs back in? What is your app's performance on 3G and in poor connectivity coverage areas? Run tests for similar extreme situations.

Although, there are other things to look out for but these are the ones you can check now.

App Review - iOS Certification Process
Once you have submitted your app, it will go through an app store review and certification process. This is to ensure

it conforms to all set rules, works well, and is not intentionally harmful.

You can go to <u>App Review Guidelines</u> and see the most current guidelines Apple® use to review your app.

If you are certain that your apps conform to these guidelines, navigate to the **project settings** by clicking on the root node of your app project within the file navigator.

Once you are done, click on the **Build Settings** button, and go down to the **Code Signing** area.

Select the **iOS Distribution** setting, which automatically selects the Distribution Signing Identity. However, if you have a setup of many distribution signing IDs, it would be required of you to choose the particular ID you wish to use.

We shall now set up a Release build and submit it to the Apple® App Store.
Select **iOS Device** as the destination of the deployment.

Select **Archive** from the **Product menu item**.

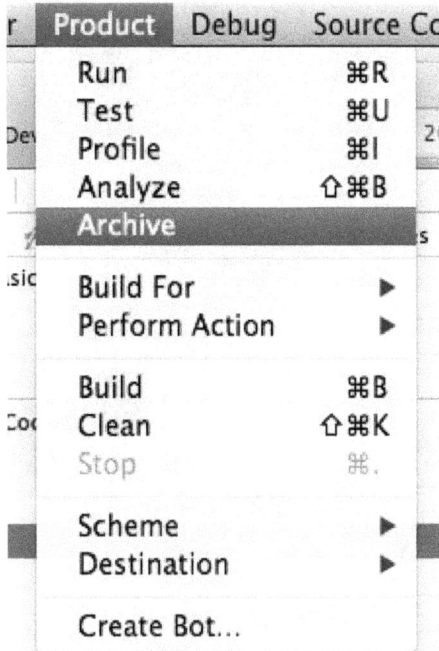

Your app archive is now up and the Xcode Organizer will be activated with the display of all the previously created archives.

Prior to submitting the app with Xcode within the Xcode Organizer, you will first need to create your App Store

---

listing in the **iTunes Connect portal**. This listing will bear all the app's information.

CHAPTER FOUR

Creating an app listing in iTunes Connect Portal

Apple® iTunes Connect Portal is different from the iOS Provisioning Portal with which you are familiar. It is a portal that ensures effective management of your apps and contracts. It also helps you evaluate your App Store performance through generated reports. Your access to the iTunes Connect Portal is automatically created at the time of your enrollment in the iPhone developer program.

Let us continue by clicking **Manage Your Apps**.

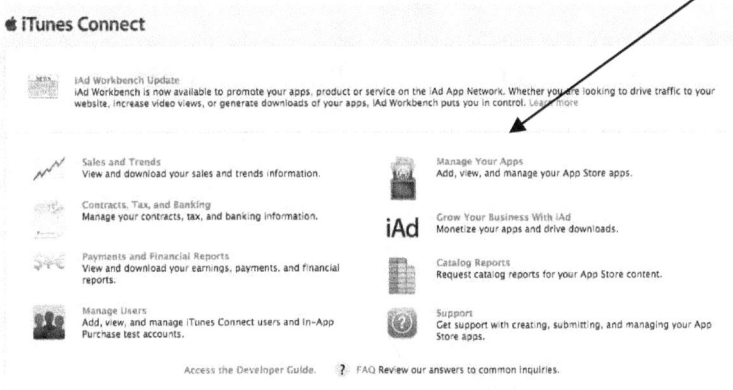

On the next page that appears, click on the blue-colored
Add
New App button.

 iTunes Connect

Add New App	Manage Your Apps

Recent Activity

iOS App Recent Activity

Select the type of App you want to upload. Here, we are uploading an iOS app.

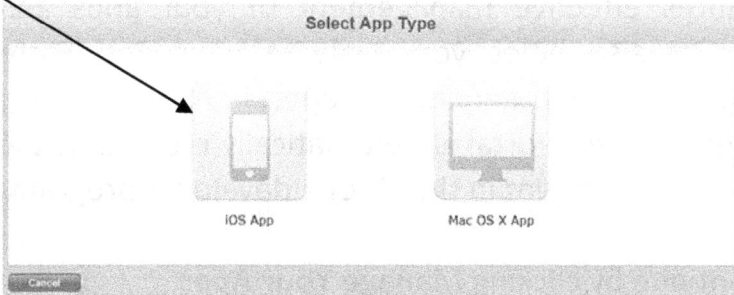

Select App Type

iOS App   Mac OS X App

Cancel

App Data.

Here, you will need to enter your app's information. When you are done, click on continue.

App Information

Enter the following information about your app.

Default Language	English
App Name	My App Test
SKU Number	
Bundle ID	My App – com. myapp

You can register a new Bundle ID here.

Pricing and Availability of App

Once your app has been certified, you may wish to make it available immediately or at a future date. If you want instant availability, simply leave the date set to the current day. At the certification stage, the app will become available (normally 24 hours after certification) in the App Store if the availability date has expired. However, if you prefer to make it available at a future date after the certification, you can set the future date.

So, choose when you want to make your app available and the price you want to sell it. When you are done, select **"continue"**

If your app is not for Free, choose "paid" under "price tier and follow the steps below:

1.   Request contracts by clicking on **"Request"** for the iOS Paid Applications contract type and click on **"done"**.

After reading the agreement, check the box and click on "**Submit**"

You will see the "**iOS Paid Applications**" contract shown under "contracts in process". Set up the Contact info, Bank Info and Tax info.

Master Agreements

Contracts In Process

Once you complete setup and the effective date has been reached, the contract will be moved to the Contracts In Effect section.

Contract Region	Contract Type	Contract Number	Contact Info	Bank Info	Tax Info	Download	Status
All (See Contract)	iOS Paid Applications	MS106109083	Set Up	Set Up	Set Up	Download Agreement	Pending Tax, Bank, Contact

Create the Contact Info:
- Click on **Set Up**
- Click on **Add New Contact**, fill in the contact details, and click on **Save**.

Note: Contacts must not have iTunes Connect accounts. You only need to select people who are capable of handling your legal, financial, and/or administrative/marketing issues that may arise from the sale of your apps on the Apple® App Store platform. Repeat this step to set up other contacts.
- Designate individual responsibilities to these contacts by choosing their names from the Contact drop down menus. When you are done, click **Done**.

To set up your bank information (so you can receive money for apps sold).

Linking your Bank account to receive payments from Apple® for your sold apps:

- For a fresh addition, click **Set Up.** But if you want to amend an already existing bank account info, click **Edit.**
  - Click the drop down menu and select an existing bank account info you want to edit. If you are adding new bank account info, **Add Bank Account.**

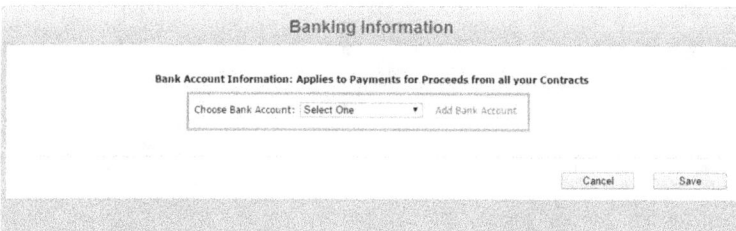

- For a fresh addition of bank account info, you will need to complete or provide the following details: bank account details, bank sort/swift code , country location of your bank branch. After providing info for each step, click **Next.**

  Note: You can get detailed information on how to set up your banking details by clicking here and scrolling to the **Banking** section.
- Next step is to choose your new bank details from the **Select a different Bank Account** option, then click **Save.**

Setting up your Tax Info:
- Click on **Set Up.**
  * Fill the tax forms as applicable to you and click **Done.**

Note: <u>Click here</u> and navigate to the **Tax** section for detailed information of tax forms.

The next thing is to fill in information about your version, copyright, categories etc.

App Metadata, EULA, Contact, Art Assets and Version Information

This is the page that contains most of your app information. You can understand better what you should enter in each box by clicking on the small question mark beside each of the boxes.

Version Number : This is exactly the same as the version number contained your app's project information settings.

Copyright : This can take the following format - "2015 Code By Mark." Just change the name and year to your own details.

Description: This is the information shown beside your app in the iTunes App Store. You must make sure your description is as detailed as possible without misleading people. If you are found to have included any misleading information, you will not be certified. For instance, if you have an app on Angry Birds, do not go describing the app in such a way that will make people start thinking it is the real game.

Rating: You will see your app rating once you have answered the questions posed to you.

Primary and Secondary Categories: Choose the most suitable category for your app.

Keywords: Enter all the keywords for which you want your app to rank highly. Because of the 100 characters limit, it is advisable not to waste your characters. Use commas instead of spaces to separate keywords. Also, ensure you research and use enough suitable keywords you can find in your specialization. There are many Apple® Store keyword research tools available if you need to explore them.

Privacy Policy, Marketing, and Support URLs: This is perhaps a landing, sales, or web page containing all your app details. This is also where you automatically send people who wish to learn more about your app.

Contact Details: This is your current contact details where any app reviewer can reach you if need be.

Uploads: Make sure that the art assets for your app listing are available in the App Store. You can find the recommended measurements for your assets by clicking the small question mark icon. You can even make use of the iOS Simulator to create your screenshots. Simply open your app within the simulator and press CMD + S; this will automatically save the screenshot to your computer desktop.

Demo Account and Reviewer Notes: Make provision for a demo account. This will make it easier for a reviewer to use and assess your app better. It is discouraging if the reviewer has to sign up before he/she can review your app. Make sure you provide clear and detailed login instructions.

You are almost done. All you need to do now is to click on "done" and your app will be published.

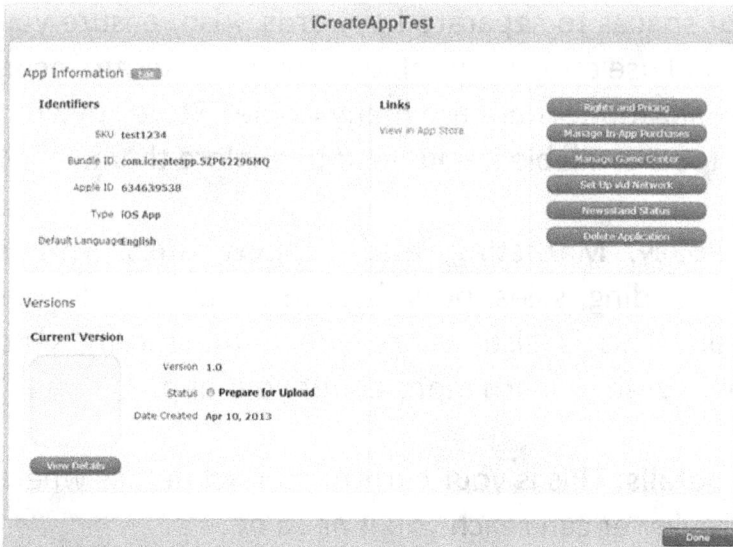

Access the app information by clicking on the app icon. From the top right hand corner, locate and click the blue button "**Ready to Upload Binary**" to answer some questions.

You may be presented with any question but currently, the question borders on whether your app has any third party content, encryption, and/or if you are making use of Adverstising Identifier.

Third party content: If you have included content you do not own originally, select **Yes**. An example is an app that shows Vimeo videos.

Encryption: If you did not make use of Objective-C libraries for data encryption, and you do not have any written code that supports encryption, select **No.**

Advertising Identifier: If at this stage you are confused about what Advertising Identifier means, it simply means you did not use it, so select **No.** However, if you bought your source code, it should come with it, so make the necessary inquiries.

Next, click the **Save** button and the app status will change to
Waiting For Upload.

Version   1.0

Status   ◎ **Waiting For Upload**

Date Created

We will now execute the final step using the **Xcode 5** developer tools.

CHAPTER FIVE

App submission using Xcode

Make sure that the status of your app has changed to **Waiting For Upload** before you continue with this step. If it has not changed, go back and click the **Save** button to change the status to **Waiting For Upload.**

Once you confirm that your app status is correct, open the Organizer in Xcode 5 by going through Windows -> Organizer. You can also open the Organizer by using the shortcut keys SHIFT+CMD+2.

Navigate to your **Archives** tab and choose the archive you previously created for upload.

Next, click on **Distribute.** This will also process the validation.
Sign in with your iTunes Connect login details, which will verify that you have an equivalent App Listing.

If everything is okay, it will initiate the binary upload for certification.

On successful upload of the binary, confirm from your iTunes Connect portal that your app status has changed to **Waiting for Review.**

It may take a few days to a week for your app to be reviewed. Do not bother checking the status every day because once the review is done, you will get an e-mail notification of the status change. Apps do not always get approved on the first review. You can be successful on your first try, but if you are not, do not get discouraged especially if you have a complex app. If you fail the review, they will usually let you know where you need to make some improvements. Simply make these adjustments, update the version number, and re-upload the binary for a second review.

CHAPTER SIX

Some common mistakes in the Apple® app submission and ways of preventing them.

It can be tiring and discouraging for a developer when a submitted app does not get approval after the first try. As much as we all want minimal rejections, there are still some mistakes that developers make, which prevents their apps from getting approval for the App Store.

There are several mistakes that can prevent your app from getting listed on the App Store. We will look at the common ones.
- Errors from Application Loader
- Incorrect use of the Advertising Identifier (IDFA)
- Mistakes from iTunes Connect
- Illegal/malicious content detected during a manual review of your app.

Let us now evaluate each of these and determine why they are constituted errors.

1. Errors due to Incorrect usage of the Advertising Identifier (IDFA)

When you are about uploading a new binary in iTunes Connect, you will be required to provide some information about your intention for the use of ads and encryption.

If you have no intention of using Facebook or ads, make sure you click the **NO** radio button as indicated here. Also note that you can still click the **NO** radio button if you are making use of only iAds. This is because Apple® iAds do not need any IDFA.

Advertising Identifier

Does this app use the Advertising Identifier (IDFA)?

○ Yes
⦿ No

The Advertising Identifier (IDFA) is a unique ID for each iOS device and is the only way to offer targeted ads. Users can choose to limit ad targeting on their iOS device.

However, if you incorporated Facebook or ads, click **Yes** and proceed to complete the lower part of the form.

Advertising Identifier

Does this app use the Advertising Identifier (IDFA)?

⦿ Yes
○ No

The Advertising Identifier (IDFA) is a unique ID for each iOS device and is the only way to offer targeted ads. Users can choose to limit ad targeting on their iOS device.

If your app is using the Advertising Identifier, check your code—including any third-party code—before you submit it to make sure that your app uses the Advertising Identifier only for the purposes listed below and respects the Limit Ad Tracking setting. If you include third-party code in your app, you are responsible for the behavior of such code, so be sure to check with your third-party provider to confirm compliance with the usage limitations of the Advertising Identifier and the Limit Ad Tracking setting.

This app uses the Advertising Identifier to (select all that apply):

☐ Serve advertisements within the app

☐ Attribute this app installation to a previously served advertisement

☐ Attribute an action taken within this app to a previously served advertisement

If you think you have another acceptable use for the Advertising Identifier, contact us.

Limit Ad Tracking setting in iOS

☐ I confirm that this app, and any third party that interfaces with this app, uses the Advertising Identifier checks and honors a user's Limit Ad Tracking setting in iOS and, when it is enabled by a user, this app does not use Advertising Identifier, and any information obtained through the use of the Advertising Identifier, in any way other than for "Limited Advertising Purposes" as defined in the iOS Developer Program License Agreement.

1. If you are making use of ads, tick the **Serve advertisements within the app** checkbox.
2. If you are using Facebook, or your app's installation originates from a cross-advertising app, tick the second checkbox.
3. Lastly, tick the checkbox marked **Limit Ad Tracking setting in iOS**.

2.   Mistakes from iTunes Connect

This is another error that is easy to rectify. An example of this error is when you omit the addition of a screenshot or any other data. You can rectify this with a simple amendment in iTunes Connect, which enable you resubmit your binary without a second upload.
Sometimes, Apple® may send you an e-mail showing displeasure about Push Notification entitlements. You can ignore this.

3. Illegal/malicious content detected during a human review of your app.

The final review of your submitted app is from a real person. Apple® has several teams of reviewers in its employ and some are more meticulous than others. Your app will be rejected by a human reviewer if it is among Apple® list of unacceptable contents such as adult content, poor-quality apps, websites disguised as apps, bugs etc.

If your app is rejected because of a bug issue, you are advised to request a "console log" from Apple® to see where the bug error is detected.

4.   Broken Links

If you have links in your app, they must all be functioning. You need to provide a link to user support with your current contact information for all your apps. You also need to provide a link to your privacy policy if you are offering auto-renewable or free subscriptions or if your apps belongs to the kids category.

5. Placeholder content in your apps

If your apps contains placeholder content, it means they will not be distributed nor approved. Therefore, your images and texts need to be finalized before you send it for reviews.

6. Insufficient information

Make sure all the details required for app review are entered into the App Review Information area of iTunes Connect. Some of the features required you signing in to access it, make sure you supply an active demo account username and password. Sometimes, there are specific configurations to set, ensure you include them. If your app features need special hardware or an environment that is difficult to reproduce, you will need to supply a demo video for it. Complete your contact information appropriately.

7. Incorrect app descriptions

App description is very important and you need to provide accurate descriptions that suits your app. The same goes for your screenshots, they need to be clear and appropriate. It will help users to better understand your app and give them a real good app store feel.

8.   Misinforming users

Your app must provide all the functions you advertised, otherwise it will give users the impression that your app is a scam. It needs to deliver all the things it is created to do.

9.   Submitting the similar app continuously

Do not submit the same app several times. It can tie up the App review process and can lead to your app being rejected. You can combine your apps together to give users a great experience.

10.   Insufficient lasting value

If your app lacks high quality content, low functionality or appeals to a small group of people, it may be rejected. Before you develop your app, you need to conduct an in-depth research to make sure that your audience size is large. You can also check your app's category on the App store to check available apps and build on them to provide a better user experience.

11.   Inferior user interface

Apple® loves a high quality, neat, refined and user friendly interface. Ensure that your user interface meets these requirements. You can check the design guides and user design do's and don'ts before you create your app.

LAST COMMENTS

Getting your app certified and published on the Apple® App Store is fun and rewarding. Once your app is live on the App Store, you will want to check your apps download/sales statistics to evaluate how the app is performing.

After the initial certification, future updates to the app will be easier to get certification approvals, especially if the updates are minimal.